Where The Dust Settles

Chloe Classen

BookLeaf Publishing

India | USA | UK

Made with ❤ on the BookLeaf Publishing Platform
www.bookleafpub.in
www.bookleafpub.com

Dedication

To those who live straddling two worlds—
one in memory, one in the now—
may you find gentle hands
to guide you
into the present.
To those who hold their breath
at the border of what was,
may you exhale and remember
you're allowed to take up space.
I dedicate these poems to you,
in the hope that you too,
will learn to dance
in the presence of
our ghosts.

Preface

Sometimes, we carry storms in our chests
and people call it "too much,"
a volume unfit for dinner tables
or Sunday mornings.
But what if "too much"
was simply truth,
wanting to spill into empty hands
that could finally hold it?
This collection is a mirror of that spill—
raw, winding, never polite.
It's a roadmap through CPTSD,
with all its corners and curves:
flashbacks in the night,
tears in unlikely places,
and a stubborn seed of hope
that refuses to die.
This is not a linear story—
you'll find light and darkness
dancing back and forth
with whiplash abandon.
If you choose to walk these pages with me,
let your voice be just as unashamed.

Content Notice (16+):

Inside these poems, you may encounter
references to sexual assault,
chronic illness,
thoughts of self-harm,
paranoia,
and other moments that shake the spirit.
Please tread softly
and take care of your heart.

Acknowledgements

To Mom and Dad,
who gave me the time
to unlearn
and relearn
how to exist:
Thank you for believing in me
when my own hope ran dry,
for opening doors
and sitting beside me
in waiting rooms,
for letting me be quiet
when words failed.
You've shown me that love
doesn't demand perfection,
only presence.
I offer these pages,
trembling but true,
in gratitude
for the safety you built
under your roof
and within your hearts.

And to Nick,
my lighthouse in the darkest nights—

thank you for holding my hand
when I couldn't keep hold of myself.
You've been the steady ground
beneath my trembling steps,
the open arms
when I've needed to crumble.
In every storm,
you are the whisper that reminds me
I can rest in this whirlwind
and still find a way
to breathe.
For all the times
I wanted to give up on tomorrow,
you believed in a new day
bright enough for both of us.
Thank you for showing me
that home isn't a place,
but the person
who sees every messy piece of you
and loves you more because of it.

The Cracks In The Wall

The cracks in the wall were the only honest things in the
room.
They didn't pretend to care.
They didn't promise escape.
They just stared back,
splintered and still,
waiting for me to fall apart.

And I did—
again and again.

I told myself they weren't prison bars,
just innocent fractures in light blue paint.
But I knew better:
I was the prisoner,
I was the guard,
and I was the fool who walked into this house
and stayed.

I counted the cracks because I couldn't count anything
else—
not your flushed cheeks,
not the heat of your breath,
not the silence between us,

damp and heavy,
pressing closer,
as if the air itself could pin me down.

The walls became accomplices.
They didn't have to hold me down—
your presence did that for them.

I begged the cracks to let me out.
"There's no place like home," I whispered,
but even they pitied me.
You cannot go home, they said.
You don't have one anymore.

So I memorized them.
I traced their jagged lines,
a distraction from the screaming in my mind—
but it wasn't enough.

I screamed anyway.
At the walls.
At the girl who stayed.
What kind of coward counts cracks in the wall
instead of running for the door?
What kind of fool stares at fractures,
thinking they'll hold her together?

I hate her.
I hate her silence,
her paralysis,
her willingness to survive
by disappearing.

She made me—
this broken thing,
this fractured shape of who I could have been.
She froze, and now I carry her weight.
Her fear.
Her failure.

I try to drown her in my anger.
I try to scream her out of my chest.
But she refuses to die.

Instead, I die for her.
Every time I feel the ghost of your breath
settling on my skin,
every time I see that soulless blue wall in my dreams,
I relive it all.
And I crack, like the walls did.

I blame her because it's easier than blaming you.
I blame her because she's weaker than me.
I blame her because forgiveness feels

impossible.

But deep down,
I know I'm still her.

A 7 Year Old Wishing On The Brightest Star In The Universe

Daddy, you are the brightest star in my sky.
When I wonder how big God must be,
I think of you—
your arms so strong, your voice so steady—
and I know He must be even greater.
But you are the proof that He exists.

One day, I want to marry young
and build what you and Mommy built,
a home sturdy enough to hold the chaos.

The world outside is sharp and loud,
but you are the unbroken note
that keeps the song from unraveling.
I know I cannot stop the changing—
this body will outgrow your arms,
this heart will stretch beyond
sleeping on your floor when I'm scared.

I am sorry for it.
I'd stop it if I could,

fold myself small to stay here forever.
The world is full of things you can't control,
and one day I will be one of them.
When I grow loud, or strange, or far away,
please don't think it's because you failed.
When the world conspires against me—
boys with their careless mouths,
life with its careless teeth—
don't panic. Don't blame yourself.
I don't.

The world is changing,
but I know you'll always be
my place to hide when the noise is too much.
You can't make it less scary,
but you are the place where fear rests.
I am afraid of everything
but losing you.

One day, I'll move out,
and the dinners at midnight
and the endless Olive Garden meals
will fade into memories.
When the world changes so much
that I don't recognize myself,
I hope you still do.
I hope you don't mourn the girl I was,

but love the woman I become.

Even when I am too big for your arms,
I will never outgrow your heart.
The world will shift and break,
but you—you are my constant.
Wherever I go, I will always be
the little girl who looked up
and saw you shining—
the brightest star
in the universe.

Love Is Not

Love is not
violent.
Violation.
Fear.
Imprisonment.

It is not
handcuffs and bruises,
guns or roses,
a hollow word whispered
to keep someone still.

Love is not
violent.
Violation.
A crime.
It does not grow in the shadow
of *stop* and *no.*
It does not bloom
when watered by tears.

Love is not
violent.
Violation.

A kink.
Owed.
It does not reside
where it was not invited.

It is not
something you can force,
something you can take,
something you can fake
to feel safe.

Love is not
violent.
Violation.

Love is not
what you did to me.

The Shell

I used to be proud of my creative mind,
my love, my passion, my independence—
the joy I felt in simply being.
My best traits were always the ones
that made me feel whole—
not perfect, just beautifully human.

I remember when my parents prayed for me,
their hands clasped tightly,
believing I was too good to fail.
They gave me everything I wanted, honestly.
Back then, my biggest problem was hating multiplication
or cleaning up my toys after building worlds
across the floor.

But simplicity never lasts.

I got sick a lot as a kid, like many do—
strep throat, headaches, fevers.
And my mom always took care of me.
But when I became "a woman,"
it was as if I wasn't supposed to need her anymore.

I wasn't their little girl anymore.

I was homeschooled, isolated,
and when I asked for help,
Mom's voice turned distant:
"You'll be fine. I used to get horrible cramps too."
Dad's tone sharpened:
"You always seem to be sick when it's convenient."
And suddenly, I was alone in that pain.

No one tells you how many times it takes
before they stop holding your hand when you're sick.
No one tells you how quickly
"Can you get me water?"
becomes greedy,
instead of a plea for help.

With each passing day,
my body betrayed me more and more.

My mind?
It feels like a foreign world,
dark and strange,
and I'm supposed to want to stay in it?
To appreciate it?
I don't know how.

Every day, I feel like I'm being rewritten—

not by my own hands.
My brain sends signals I didn't approve of.
And when I beg it to stop,
it tells me:
"You're faking it for attention."

It becomes a monster,
a mutation of everything I feared in the world.
A world where I am at war with myself,
fighting against the voices that say I am too much,
not enough,
a shadow of who I was meant to be.

In this battle,
I've started to believe
I'm not worth healing.
Maybe I'll always be like this—
lost in fragments of someone
I can barely recognize.

The pieces of me are scattered,
and I'm made of medicine and frozen food,
just trying to survive,
clinging to whatever remnants of hope I can find.
I want to be free,
but I don't know how anymore.

Here I am,
caught between wanting to rest
and wishing for a life I can't reach.
I'm not in bed because I'm lazy,
or because I let myself fall apart.
I'm here because I am exhausted
from battling every single part of me.

I've fought for so long,
but all I've got left is the shell
of someone I used to be.

My Ghosts And I

I see two ghosts of myself in the mirror.

One, perfectly imperfect:
beautiful, loved,
singing songs that left the crowd breathless.
Everyone adored me—
especially myself.

The other, imperfectly perfect:
awkward, disliked,
her songs cracking into croaks and tears.
The weight of her failed potential
left the crowd in silence.
Everyone hated her—
especially herself.

I don't know which was real.
Maybe both.
Maybe neither.

Whichever it was, they linger,
haunting the edges of my mind.
One whispers, *"You'll never be her again."*
The other hisses, *"You'll always be me."*

And I believe them both.

I imagine the end:
the world reduced to ash,
nothing left but the quiet.

When the apocalypse comes,
and the ghosts of who I was
meet the shell of who I am,
maybe then we'll find peace.

Maybe they'll dissolve into one.
No ghosts.
No burdens.
No comparisons.

Just me,
at last,
at rest.

In The Eye Of The Storm

Through depressive storms,
he stands beside me,
steady as a lighthouse.

His hand in mine is the anchor
that keeps me from floating away.
Even as the winds howl,
he whispers calm into my chaos—
a language I barely understand,
but cling to anyway.

We sit together in the wreckage of my mind,
his presence cutting through the fog.
He doesn't try to fix me,
doesn't try to stop the storm.
He just stays,
until the skies turn blue again.

I call it love.
He calls it weathering the storm.
Together, we find the eye.

Pain Is

Pain is the way your eyes burn when you're tired.
The way you're tired,
no matter how long you sleep.
The way you sleep all day,
but wake up
to the same dull ache that held you hostage before.

Pain is the pill you take
to stop the tossing and turning,
to quiet the nightmares of him.

It is waking up
and remembering it wasn't just a dream,
but a memory.

Pain is fearing people.
Needing people.
Fearing that you need them.

It's feeling unloved, unwanted, unseen.
It's not knowing yourself,
or believing in yourself,
or believing yourself.

Pain is waiting for yourself to fail,
begging everyone else
to prove you wrong.
It's the numbness of giving up,
and the sting of knowing you're right.

And it is more than this:
the unspoken,
the physical.
Pain is forgetting to write down the way it grinds your
body
into something small,
fragile.

It's the silent betrayal of your body—
your shoulders, your joints, your back—
the places you never wanted to name
because naming them means they're real.

Pain is all of it.
Not one sharp wound,
but every layer stacked on top of each other,
until you can't tell where one ends
and the next begins.

Love, Always

I feel heavy in my sickness,
but in your support, I feel lighter.
The fear of rejection, the doubt I carry,
melts away when I lean into your arms.

I wish I could go back,
tell my younger self it would get easier—
not in body,
not in mind,
but in knowing you would always be there.

You would be the steady hand holding me
when my strength faltered.
You would love me in my weakness
and whisper that I am enough.

As a child, I thought you had it all figured out.
I believed you knew everything,
that you were perfect—
but you didn't, and that's okay.

You grew with me.
You were not stagnant,
but always evolving, always learning.

You have been my mirror,
reflecting love, patience, and grace,
even when I couldn't see it myself.

I've never known two people more willing to admit their
flaws,
to say, *"We don't understand your pain,
but we're here."*
You pushed me to face what hurt,
to grow beyond it.
And when you couldn't understand,
you trusted me to guide you.
You trusted in the strength
we built together.

I am happy to say,
I grew away before I grew up.
And now, as I stand grown,
I stand reconciled.

We are no longer just parent and child.
You are my best friends,
my pillars of wisdom,
my heart's home.

Even when I can't find pride in myself,
you remind me that you are proud of me.

And those words—
they are the rope I cling to
on days I can't breathe for myself.

Thank you for seeing me,
for holding me,
for never turning away.
You've shown me that love is not a place,
but a feeling I carry with me—
always.

The Scorekeeper

We met when I was already in a low place.
You took a bad situation
and made it worse.

You slipped in under the guise
of being less than the worst thing
that had ever happened to me.
Amid the fear of him,
you offered a distraction,
flaunting promises of peace and answers—
all while plotting
to tear me apart, piece by piece.

And here you are,
four years after him,
still torturing me.
Worse than he ever was.

Yes, he violated my body,
but you do too—
every day,
as long as I can remember.
You evolve into new monsters,
dodging my defenses,

and I know
I will never be strong enough
to escape you
the way I escaped him.

I believed the diagnosis
would give the doctors answers.
Instead, it uncovered only more questions.
No medicine can leash you.
No habits can help me outrun you.

And while I knew
you would weaponize his trauma,
I never imagined the day
I learned my illness
was born of it.
That was harder
than any day with him.

You, my body—
you betrayed me.
You kept the score.
Not to protect me,
but to hurt me.

I scream.
I beg.

Release me from this torture device,
this intimate betrayer
that sends flashbacks to weaken my mind,
that stops my body altogether
to prevent me from moving on.

I imagine a day—
a miracle, a fantasy—
when I am free.
Fully and correctly diagnosed.
The incurable pain,
the complex symptoms—
treated, tamed,
gone.

In this world,
I am normal.

I go to class.
I exercise.
I work.
I sing again.
I can simply take a walk.

Finally,
I am capable of everything
you and he

stole from me.

But that's just my imagination.

Off Note

Synchronized, dull conversation—
my ears ring in the silence of my voice.

I speak.
An off note
interrupts the choir,
a dissonance they never asked for.

Their harmony sways but doesn't falter,
a tide pushing me gently
back into silence.

I hear it now:
my story,
unwelcome.

Not here.
Not now.

But still, it hums beneath the surface,
discordant and raw.
The off note lingers,
stretching into a chord
they cannot unhear.

One day, I think,
it will shatter their harmony.

Teach Me How

We meet regularly for brunch
in our haunted mansion.
We go there because very few do—
no one else dares to step inside.

The mansion remembers us.
Its walls are layered with our post-its,
yellow notes clinging to cracked plaster,
whispering:
This is no longer our home.
But still, the ghosts linger.
They watch us from the corners,
perplexed by how we've learned to stay.

The dust falls like snow,
soft, relentless,
and we laugh—
because no one else sees
the magic in that.

We dance for the mansion's residents—
those who, since dead,
cannot dance for themselves.
Our feet stir the dust into clouds,

and we breathe it in,
turning their grief into light.

We joke that maybe
we are the skeletons
in their closets—
the ones who learned to sing
in the face of silence,
to twirl through the pain
that kept us chained.

And as the snow falls,
I fall the same—
in love with your soul.
Not for its perfection,
but for the way it shines
in places where light should not exist.

I've never seen someone
dance through
what we went through.

Teach me how.

Walking By Candlelight

I think of the dark,
the small radius where candlelight reaches.
I imagine someone navigating caves or catacombs,
lost beneath a palace,
afraid of what lies beyond the glow.

It's the uncertainty of life—
I see only what is directly in front of me,
while the shadows beyond
could hold monsters, dragons, beasts.
Or perhaps a garden,
a magical underground lake,
something beautiful, waiting.

Though the potential is equal for good, bad, or neither,
I spend my nearly blind walk
fearing only the bad.

I want to live differently:
to savor the dull,
to seek the good,
to face the bad only when it steps into the light.

But not like this—

not a life where the neutral is spent in fear,
where the good is overshadowed
by how fleeting it feels.

Sometimes, I wish I could blow the candle out entirely—
walk blindly, moment to moment,
instead of casting spells,
begging gods
to stretch the light across the room.

I wish to trust the shadows,
to embrace the unknown,
to find peace without sight.

I wish for silence in my restless mind,
to finally set down the candle,
feel the cool stone beneath my feet,
and walk unafraid into the dark.

Arachnophobia

I am small,
tucked into the corners of your walls,
always lurking, unseen.

Your house is warm,
and I give you my all,
keeping the pests at bay.
It is mutual—
so long as I remain hidden,
so long as I stay still.

When I am hidden,
it is easy to forget your disgust.
You might even find beauty in me:
fragile,
worthy of gentle care.

But when I move,
when I'm exposed,
your gaze shifts.
You see my limbs, long and intrusive,
my presence, too close to your face.
I am a creature of too many legs,
too many eyes.

Ugly, you think.
Poisoned.

You gag at the sight of me.
I disgust you,
not for what I do,
but for what I am.

Perhaps that's why I scream to the world:
"I am intolerable,
and I embrace that."

But the truth is,
I don't want to invade your home.
I want you to see my resilience—
to look at me as I am:
beautiful,
unashamed.

This is not about spiders.

Please remember:
I am not violating you
simply because I have been violated.
Rape is not contagious.

The Cage

I built a cage,
thinking it would keep me safe.
Its bars were made of reasons:
They'll hurt you again.
You'll fall apart.
Excuses, really,
to hide from the world.

At first, it was comforting—
a quiet place to rest,
to be small.
But over time,
I outgrew it.
The bars, once protective,
became suffocating.

The cage held me still,
but you stepped inside anyway.
You didn't tear it down.
You didn't tell me
I had to leave.

Instead, you sat with me.
You folded your legs on the cold floor

and waited.

I was ashamed of my mess.
The way I paced like an animal,
snapping at the bars
but never daring to break them.

But you never flinched.
You reached for my hand,
even when it trembled,
even when it hurt to hold.

You showed me that cages
aren't always prisons—
sometimes they are sanctuaries.
And when I was ready,
you opened the door
and walked out with me.

Medusa: The Scorekeeper Revisited

They called her a monster,
but I think she was just tired.
Tired of men who never asked permission,
tired of gods who claimed worship
while taking what they wanted.

Maybe she wanted peace—
but peace was never meant for her.
She learned to wield rage
like a sword,
her hair a crown of venom,
her eyes a defense sharper than any blade.

They turned her victims to stone,
but I wonder if they also froze
her grief, her exhaustion.
A punishment not for what she'd done,
but for what had been done to her.

I know her well,
this Medusa,
her legend twisted by those
who only saw her teeth.

I am her mirror,
but instead of serpents,
I have scars—
some that heal,
some that keep hissing.

They told me to turn my gaze away.
They said my body—
its chronic pain, its trauma—
was too ugly to confront.
Too much to bear.

But I see beauty in the cracks.
I see resilience in her venom.
I see survival where they saw only rage.

Let them call me a monster.
Let them avert their eyes.
They don't know what it means
to endure,
to protect what's left,
to carry a curse that wasn't mine
but became my armor.

I am Medusa,

and I will not apologize
for the score I keep.

Love Is

Love is a steady hand
that doesn't flinch at trembling fingers.
It is an open door,
even when you're too afraid to knock.

It's a language you don't have to speak,
a song you can hum when the words escape you.

Love is not the absence of chaos—
it's the calm within it.
The place where the storm breaks,
but you don't.

It's the warmth of meeting someone
in the eye of the storm,
and staying,
not to fix them,
but to hold them through it.

Love does not demand a version of you
that isn't real.
It doesn't polish you into something new—
it sees beauty in your fractures.

Love is a voice that whispers,
"I see you.
I hear you.
You're safe."

It is a mirror that reflects
not just who you are,
but who you're becoming—
and smiles at both.

Love is not always loud or sweeping.
Sometimes it's quiet,
gentle as a breath,
reaching you in ways
you didn't know you needed.

Love is here.
Not to save you,
but to remind you
you're worth saving.

The Path To Healing

Healing is not a straight path.
It's not a ladder to climb
or a finish line to cross.

It's a maze,
a slow stumble through overgrown trails
you thought would lead somewhere clearer.
It's circling back to the same pain
you thought you'd buried,
only to dig deeper,
find its roots,
and pull it out again.

It's waking up to the same ache,
day after day,
and choosing to get up anyway.

Healing is not progress others can see.
It's the moment you stop running,
not to quit,
but to breathe.

It's putting down the sword,
not because the fight is over,

but because you've learned
you don't have to win
to deserve peace.

It's not letting the weight of the world
keep you from holding yourself up,
but knowing when to rest.

Healing is no longer asking,
"Why did this happen to me?"
It's letting the answer go.

It's a journey, not a race.
It's a choice,
made over and over again.

Returning|Moving On

I wanted to go back.
Back to a time
before the dust settled,
when the air was still clear,
and innocence was untouched.

I thought,
if I retraced my steps,
I could rebuild it—
the girl I was before him,
before the sickness,
before the scars.

But innocence is not a thing
you can reclaim.
It slips through your hands
like smoke,
like time.

I've walked the old roads.
I've visited the places
that once held meaning,
only to find they've forgotten me.
And maybe I've forgotten them too.

The truth is,
progress is forward,
not backward.
Returning
isn't the same as healing.

And moving on
doesn't mean forgetting.
It means I carry what I've learned,
what I've lost,
what I've loved,
and walk into the future—
knowing that I cannot rebuild the past,
but I can build something new.

Forgiveness Is A House

45

Forgiveness is a house
I didn't want to build.

I wanted to live in ruins,
to stare at the wreckage,
to let it echo
with my screams.

But forgiveness,
like healing,
is a choice.
It's not a single act,
but a thousand small ones.

Forgiveness is picking up a brick,
even when your hands bleed.
It's mixing mortar from tears,
layering walls from pieces of yourself
you thought were too broken to use.

The house is not perfect.
Its roof leaks.
Its walls creak.
The ivy you planted climbs unevenly,

refusing to grow where you want it to.

Some days, it feels more like a tomb.
Other days, the flowers bloom—
not because the house is flawless,
but because it stands at all.

Forgiveness is not an apology.
It's not an erasure of pain.
It's a place where you live
with the memories
and learn how to breathe in them.

It holds my grief in its beams,
my rage in its walls.
It has rooms big enough for sorrow,
windows wide enough for joy.

And though the house is unfinished,
though the paint still peels
and the floors still creak,
it is alive.
It is mine.

Forgiveness is not a door you slam shut.
It's a threshold you cross
over and over again,

until you realize
you've built something worth staying in.

The Cadence Of Me

My voice used to come so easily.
Words, melodies,
they spilled out of me
like rivers,
always flowing.

But then the silence came.
A pause that stretched too long,
turning music to static,
melody to noise.

I tried to force the rhythm,
to find the song again—
but my voice cracked
beneath the weight of its absence.

For years, I thought I'd lost it.
That part of me that was loud,
and proud,
and so unapologetically alive.

But it was never lost.
Just quiet.
A hum beneath the surface,

waiting for me to listen.

Now, I don't sing the way I used to.
I don't fill the room
or leave the crowd breathless.
But I've found something better:

The cadence of me.

Not loud,
not perfect—
but steady.

My voice, not bursting like rivers,
but flowing like a stream.
Gentle. Persistent.
And enough.

The Scorekeeper: Finalized

I kept the score for too long.
Measured every scar,
every bruise,
every moment the world proved
it was not safe.

I counted the cracks in the wall,
the nights I begged the air to set me free.
I counted the weight of his breath on my skin,
the way my body locked me inside itself.

I tallied the silence—
the screams I swallowed,
the hours spent pacing the cage,
gripping the bars
but never breaking them.

I blamed her—
the girl who stared at fractures,
the girl who let the storm rage through her veins
and called it love.
The girl who stayed.

But she didn't fail me.

Survival wasn't silence.
It was staring at the cracks and finding patterns,
finding meaning,
finding a reason to hold on.

She didn't fail me.
She fought for me.
Not with swords,
but with the quiet refusal to stop breathing.

And now, I see her—
not a victim,
not a mistake,
but the foundation of everything I've become.

The cage is open now.
The cracks are just cracks.
The ghosts no longer haunt the mansion.
And though the scorekeeper still whispers,
I don't always listen.

But some days, I do.
Some days, I feel the weight of it all—
the breath, the silence,
the girl I was and the girl I lost.
Some days, the cage feels closed again,

and I am pacing.

But I know this:
it is not failure to stumble.
It is not failure to grieve.
It is not failure to return to the wreckage
and feel its pull.

Here is the scoreboard.
I am erasing it.
Not because I am healed,
but because healing isn't an end.

It's a beginning
I choose every day.

She was brave.
I am brave.
And we carry this together—
not to tally,
not to measure,
but to live.